Scripture Novenas

Novena of Thanksgiving

Prepared by
the Daughters of St. Paul in Brazil

Translated from the Portuguese by
Germana Santos, FSP

BOOKS & MEDIA
Boston

Texts of the New Testament used in this work are taken from *The St. Paul Catholic Edition of the New Testament,* translated by Mark A. Wauck, copyright © 1992, Society of St. Paul. All rights reserved.

Texts of the Psalms used in this work are translated by Manuel Miguens, copyright © 1995, Daughters of St. Paul.

All other Old Testament scripture quotations are from the *New Revised Standard Version Bible, Catholic Edition,* copyright © 1993 and 1989 by the Division of Christian Education of the National Council of the Churches of Christ in the U.S.A. Used by permission. All rights reserved.

ISBN 0-8198-5148-5

Original Portuguese edition: Copyright © Pie Sociedade Filhas de São Paulo—SP.

Copyright © 2000, Daughters of St. Paul

Printed and published in the U.S.A. by Pauline Books & Media, 50 Saint Pauls Avenue, Boston MA 02130-3491.

www.pauline.org

Pauline Books & Media is the publishing house of the Daughters of St. Paul, an international congregation of women religious serving the Church with the communications media.

2 3 4 5 6 7 8   06 05 04 03 02 01

What Is a Novena?

Most families have traditions—cherished customs and practices handed on from one generation to another. A novena is like that—a Catholic "family tradition," a type of prayer that is one of the ways our family of faith has prayed for centuries.

The Catholic tradition of praying novenas comes from the earliest days of the Church. After the ascension of Jesus, the Acts of the Apostles tells us that the Apostles and Mary gathered together and "devoted themselves single-mindedly to prayer" (Acts 1:14). And on the day of Pentecost, the Spirit of the Lord came to them. Based on this, Christians have always prayed for various needs, trusting that God both hears and answers prayer. Over time, the custom of praying for nine consecutive days for a particular need came to be called praying "a novena," since *novena* means *nine*.

There are many different kinds of novenas, but their purpose is the same: we call to mind our needs and we ask God's help and protection while remembering how much God loves us. And as we pray, we also ask for a greater understanding and acceptance of God's mysterious workings in our life and the lives of those we love.

"But," we might wonder, "doesn't God know our needs before we even ask; isn't praying once for something enough?" Although we believe in God's love for us, sometimes we need to remind ourselves of this. Although we know we are held in God's hands and that God will not let go, sometimes we need reassurance. In times of darkness, we need something to hold on to; in times of joy, we want to keep rejoicing! What may appear to be mere repetition in a novena is really a continual act of faith and hope in our loving God.

Like the rosary, the Stations of the Cross, the Liturgy of the Hours, or meal prayers, novenas are one small part of our Catholic faith. The greatest prayer of all is the Eucharistic Celebration. The Eucharist is central to Catholic living; from this great source flows the answer to all our human longings. Through praying with Scripture in this novena, may we draw near our Eucharistic God with confidence, "to receive mercy and find grace to help us in time of need" (Hebrews 4:16).

NOVENA OF THANKSGIVING

The blessings of God surround us daily and a thankful person is insightfully attentive to God's immense care for the world. Gratitude is one of the hallmarks of a lived Christianity; in fact, *Eucharist*, the center around which we live, means *"thanksgiving."*

As we grow in faith through prayer, we gradually begin to realize that *everything* is gift; *everything* comes to us from the generous hands of the Lord. Therefore, to praise and bless God is our natural response to all we have received: "Praise the Lord, O my soul! I will praise the Lord as long as I live; I will sing praises to my God all my life long" (Psalm 146).

As grateful children who continually recognize our Father's plan of love, we allow the joy we feel in our hearts to spill over into others' lives, as we pass on to our brothers and sisters the love we ourselves have received.

To be done on a daily basis

For nine consecutive days, set apart time for quiet reflection on the true meaning of your life. The title given to each day is the theme for that day. Try to center your meditation on the biblical thoughts suggested for the day in light of this theme, and bear in mind your own needs and desires.

Remind yourself that you are in God's presence. Ask God to bless you and all those you love as you hold in your heart the persons and intentions that you especially desire to pray for. Confidently express these intentions to God.

Pray the **Opening Prayer,** and then begin to meditate on the day's scripture passage. Allow a slow, peaceful repetition of the Word of God to nourish whatever within you may be barren and dry, anxious and afraid. Try to open your heart to hear the Lord speaking to you about your situation. Pay attention to any unexpected thoughts or feelings that arise during your prayer…is God extending any invitations to you regarding your prayer intentions?

As you come to the end of your prayer time, spend some moments silently recalling the day's theme. End your prayer time by praying an ***Our Father, Hail Mary, Glory Be,*** and the ***Closing Prayer.***

Opening Prayer
(for each day)

Eternal and all-powerful God, everything that we are and own we have received from your love and your goodness. With this prayer we wish to thank you for all the times that, because of preoccupation and worry, we failed to give you thanks. May your Word increase our desire to live in a spirit of gratitude. Through your Son, our Lord Jesus Christ, in the unity of the Holy Spirit, one God forever and ever. Amen.

Closing Prayer
(for each day)

Lord, your Word encourages us to thank you always because everything comes from you and on you everything depends. We wish to repeat, not only with our lips, but also with our every breath: "We give you thanks for everything, O Lord, for your love is everlasting." Through your Son, our Lord Jesus Christ, in the unity of the Holy Spirit, one God forever and ever. Amen.

Let Us Thank God for His Protection

Opening prayer (page 11)

For meditation

Blessed are you, O LORD, the God of our ancestor Israel, for ever and ever. Yours, O LORD, are the greatness, the power, the glory, the victory, and the majesty; for all that is in the heavens and on the earth is yours; yours is the kingdom, O LORD, and you are exalted as head above all. Riches and honor come from you…. Now, our God, we give thanks to you, and praise your glorious name.

1 Chronicles 29:10–13

To recall throughout the day

*Give thanks to the Lord for he is good,
 for his loving kindness is forever.
Let them give thanks to the Lord
 for his loving kindness
and for his wonders on behalf
 of humankind.*

Psalm 107:1, 8

Closing prayer (page 12)

LET US THANK GOD FOR HIS MERCY

Opening prayer (page 11)

For meditation

Bless God and acknowledge him in the presence of all the living for the good things he has done for you. Bless and sing praise to his name. With fitting honor declare to all people the deeds of God. Do not be slow to acknowledge him. It is good to conceal the secret of a king, but to acknowledge and reveal the works of God, and with fitting honor to acknowledge him. Do good and evil will not overtake you.

Tobit 12:6–7

"My soul gives praise to the Lord,
and my spirit rejoices in God my Savior;
because he had regard for the lowliness
   of his handmaid,
behold, henceforth all generations shall
   call me blessed,
for the Mighty One has done great things for me,
and holy is his name,
and his mercy is from generation to generation
toward those who fear him."

Luke 1:46–50

To recall throughout the day

*Give thanks to the Lord for he is good,
   for his loving kindness is forever.
Let them give thanks to the Lord
   for his loving kindness
and for his wonders on behalf
   of humankind.*

Psalm 107:1, 8

Closing prayer (page 12)

LET US THANK GOD FOR HIS PARDON

Opening prayer *(page 11)*

For meditation

All my inner self, bless his holy name.
Bless the Lord, my soul,
and let not all his kindnesses sink
   into oblivion:
it is he who forgives all your guilt;
he, who heals all your infirmities....

Psalm 103:1–3

But thanks be to God, for you who were once slaves to sin have become obedient from the heart to the pattern of teaching which was handed down to you—you have been set free from sin and have become slaves of righteousness. (I am speaking in terms suitable to the weakness of your human nature.) For just as you once allowed your bodily members to become slaves of impurity and ever greater wickedness, so now you offer your bodily members as slaves to righteousness so that they may be sanctified.

Romans 6:17–19

To recall throughout the day

Give thanks to the Lord for he is good,
*   for his loving kindness is forever.*
Let them give thanks to the Lord
*   for his loving kindness*
and for his wonders on behalf
*   of humankind.*

Psalm 107:1, 8

Closing prayer (*page 12*)

LET US THANK GOD FOR ALL HIS GOODNESS

Opening prayer *(page 11)*

For meditation

Give thanks no matter what happens, for this is God's will for you in Christ Jesus.

1 Thessalonians 5:18

I will give full-mouthed thanks to the Lord,
and praise him in public,
for he stood at the right hand of the poor
   to save his life from his judges.

Psalm 109:30–31

To recall throughout the day

Give thanks to the Lord for he is good,
*   for his loving kindness is forever.*
Let them give thanks to the Lord
*   for his loving kindness*
and for his wonders on behalf
*   of humankind.*

Psalm 107:1, 8

Closing prayer (page 12)

Christ Promised to Listen to Our Petitions

Opening prayer *(page 11)*

For meditation

"Ask! and it shall be given to you;
seek! and you shall find;
knock! and it shall be opened to you.

"For everyone who asks, will receive,
and whoever seeks, will find,
and to those who knock,
it shall be opened."

Matthew 7:7–8

"Amen, amen, I say to you, whatever you ask the Father for in my name he will give you.

Up till now you have asked for nothing in my name; ask and you will receive, so your joy may be complete."

John 16:23–24

To recall throughout the day

Give thanks to the Lord for he is good,
   for his loving kindness is forever.
Let them give thanks to the Lord
   for his loving kindness
and for his wonders on behalf
   of humankind.

Psalm 107:1, 8

Closing prayer *(page 12)*

LET US THANK YAHWEH AT ALL TIMES

Opening prayer *(page 11)*

For meditation

I will bless the Lord at all times;
his praise is constantly on my lips.
It is in the Lord that my soul shall boast.
The humble shall hear of it and rejoice.
Join me in celebrating the greatness
   of the Lord,
and let us extol his name together.
Taste and realize how good the Lord is.
Happy the person who takes refuge in him.

Psalm 34:2–4, 9

Speak to each other in psalms, hymns, and spiritual songs; sing praise to the Lord in your hearts, giving thanks always and for everything to God the Father in the name of our Lord Jesus Christ.

Ephesians 5:19–20

To recall throughout the day

*Give thanks to the Lord for he is good,
  for his loving kindness is forever.
Let them give thanks to the Lord
  for his loving kindness
and for his wonders on behalf
  of humankind.*

Psalm 107:1, 8

Closing prayer (page 12)

THE ACT OF GIVING THANKS GIVES MEANING TO LIFE

Opening prayer (page 11)

For meditation

Thus do I want to bless you throughout
   my life,
to raise my hands for the sake of your name.
Since you have become a helper for me,
I will shout joyfully in the shelter of
   your wings.
My soul is deeply attached to you;
your right hand sustains me.

Psalm 63:5, 8–9

But everything created by God is good and nothing is to be rejected when it is received with thanksgiving, for it is sanctified by the word of God and prayer.

1 Timothy 4:4–5

To recall throughout the day

Give thanks to the Lord for he is good,
 for his loving kindness is forever.
Let them give thanks to the Lord
 for his loving kindness
and for his wonders on behalf
 of humankind.

Psalm 107:1, 8

Closing prayer *(page 12)*

Let Us Thank Our Father for Having Adopted Us as His Children

Opening prayer *(page 11)*

For meditation

"Everyone who asks, receives,
and whoever seeks, will find,
and to those who knock, it shall be opened.
What man among you, if his son asked for
   a loaf, would hand him a stone?
Or if he asked for a fish,
would hand him a snake?
So if you who are evil know how
   to give good gifts to your children,
How much more will your Father in heaven
   give good things to those who ask him!"

Matthew 7:8–11

Give thanks to the Father who made you worthy to share in the portion of the saints in light. He has rescued us from the power of darkness and has brought us into the Kingdom of his beloved Son, by whom we are redeemed and our sins are forgiven.

Colossians 1:12–14

To recall throughout the day

Give thanks to the Lord for he is good,
 for his loving kindness is forever.
Let them give thanks to the Lord
 for his loving kindness
and for his wonders on behalf
 of humankind.

Psalm 107:1, 8

Closing prayer (page 12)

JESUS PRAISES GRATITUDE

Opening prayer *(page 11)*

For meditation

As he was entering a village he was met by ten lepers who stood at a distance, and they raised their voices and cried out, "Jesus, master, have mercy on us!" When he saw them he said, "Go show yourselves to the priests!" And it happened that they were made clean while they were on their way. One of them, when he saw he had been cured, returned, glorifying God in a loud voice, and he fell face down at Jesus' feet and thanked him. He was a Samaritan. In response Jesus said, "Were not ten made clean? Where, then, are the other nine?

Did no one return to give glory to God except this foreigner?" Then he said to him, "Arise and go; your faith has saved you."

Luke 17:12–19

To recall throughout the day

*Give thanks to the Lord for he is good,
    for his loving kindness is forever.
Let them give thanks to the Lord
    for his loving kindness
and for his wonders on behalf
    of humankind.*

Psalm 107:1, 8

Closing prayer *(page 12)*

Titles in the series of *Scripture Novenas:*

#0-8198-5140-X Novena for Health

#0-8198-5141-8 Novena for Families

#0-8198-5142-6 Novena in a Time of Difficulty

#0-8198-5143-4 Novena in Praise of the Father

#0-8198-5144-2 Novena in Praise of the Son

#0-8198-5145-0 Novena in Praise of the Holy Spirit

#0-8198-5146-9 Novena of Forgiveness

#0-8198-5147-7 Novena of Hope in Suffering

#0-8198-5148-5 Novena of Thanksgiving

#0-8198-5149-3 Novena to Find Employment

#0-8198-5150-7 Novena to Obtain Patience

#0-8198-5151-5 Novena to Overcome Fear

Pauline BOOKS & MEDIA

The Daughters of St. Paul operate book and media centers at the following addresses. Visit, call or write the one nearest you today, or find us on the World Wide Web, www.pauline.org

CALIFORNIA
3908 Sepulveda Blvd, Culver City, CA 90230   310-397-8676
5945 Balboa Avenue, San Diego, CA 92111   858-565-9181
46 Geary Street, San Francisco, CA 94108   415-781-5180

FLORIDA
145 S.W. 107th Avenue, Miami, FL 33174   305-559-6715

HAWAII
1143 Bishop Street, Honolulu, HI 96813   808-521-2731
Neighbor Islands call: 800-259-8463

ILLINOIS
172 North Michigan Avenue, Chicago, IL 60601   312-346-4228

LOUISIANA
4403 Veterans Memorial Blvd, Metairie, LA 70006   504-887-7631

MASSACHUSETTS
Rte. 1, 885 Providence Hwy, Dedham, MA 02026   781-326-5385

MISSOURI
9804 Watson Road, St. Louis, MO 63126   314-965-3512

NEW JERSEY
561 U.S. Route 1, Wick Plaza, Edison, NJ 08817   732-572-1200

NEW YORK
150 East 52nd Street, New York, NY 10022   212-754-1110
78 Fort Place, Staten Island, NY 10301   718-447-5071

OHIO
2105 Ontario Street, Cleveland, OH 44115   216-621-9427

PENNSYLVANIA
9171-A Roosevelt Blvd, Philadelphia, PA 19114   215-676-9494

SOUTH CAROLINA
243 King Street, Charleston, SC 29401   843-577-0175

TENNESSEE
4811 Poplar Avenue, Memphis, TN 38117   901-761-2987

TEXAS
114 Main Plaza, San Antonio, TX 78205   210-224-8101

VIRGINIA
1025 King Street, Alexandria, VA 22314   703-549-3806

CANADA
3022 Dufferin Street, Toronto, Ontario, Canada M6B 3T5   416-781-9131
1155 Yonge Street, Toronto, Ontario, Canada M4T 1W2   416-934-3440

¡También somos su fuente para libros, videos y música en español!